Swear Word Coloring Book.

The Incredibly Rude FANTASY COLORING BOOK FOR ADULTS

Swear Word Coloring Book

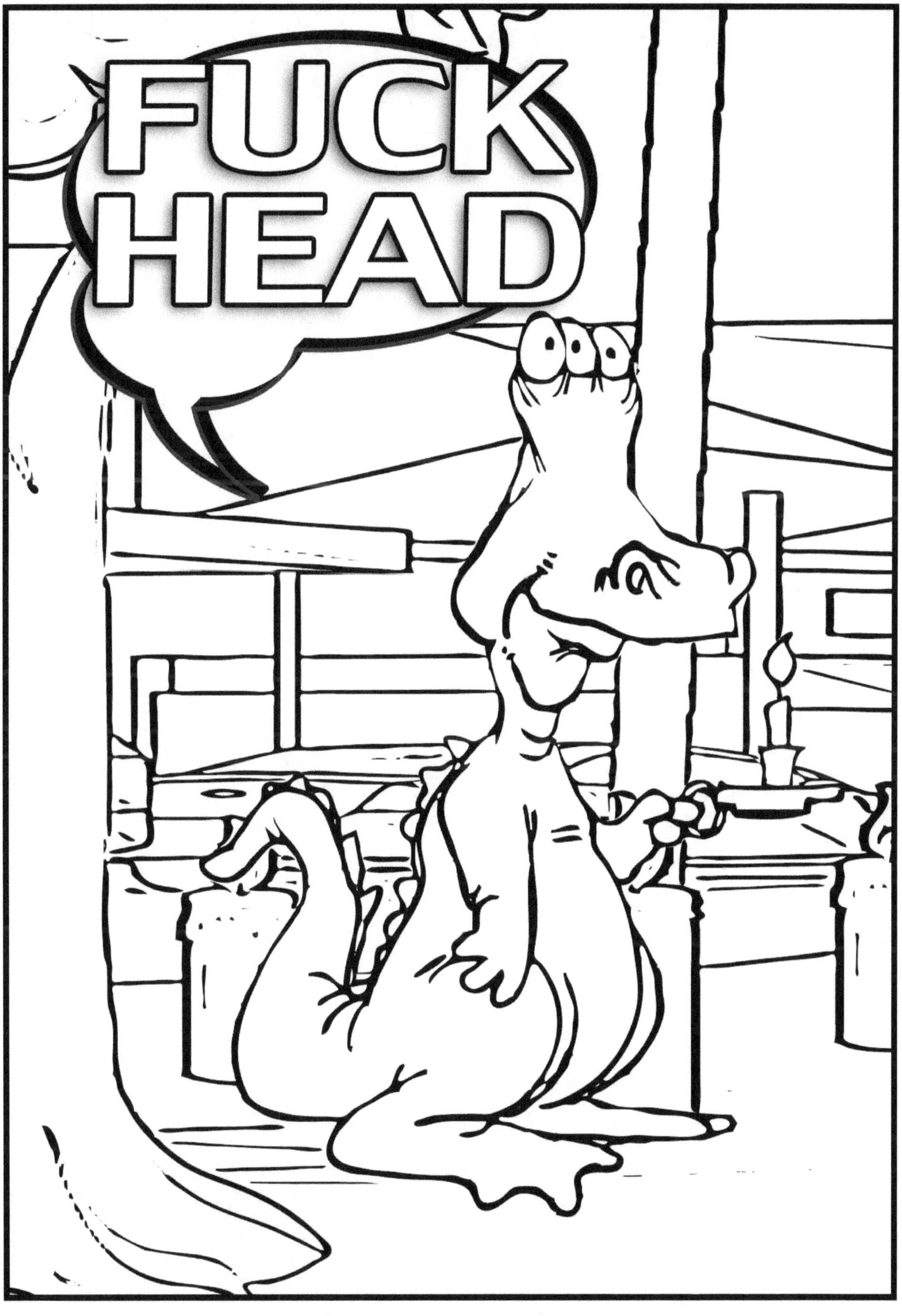
FUCK HEAD

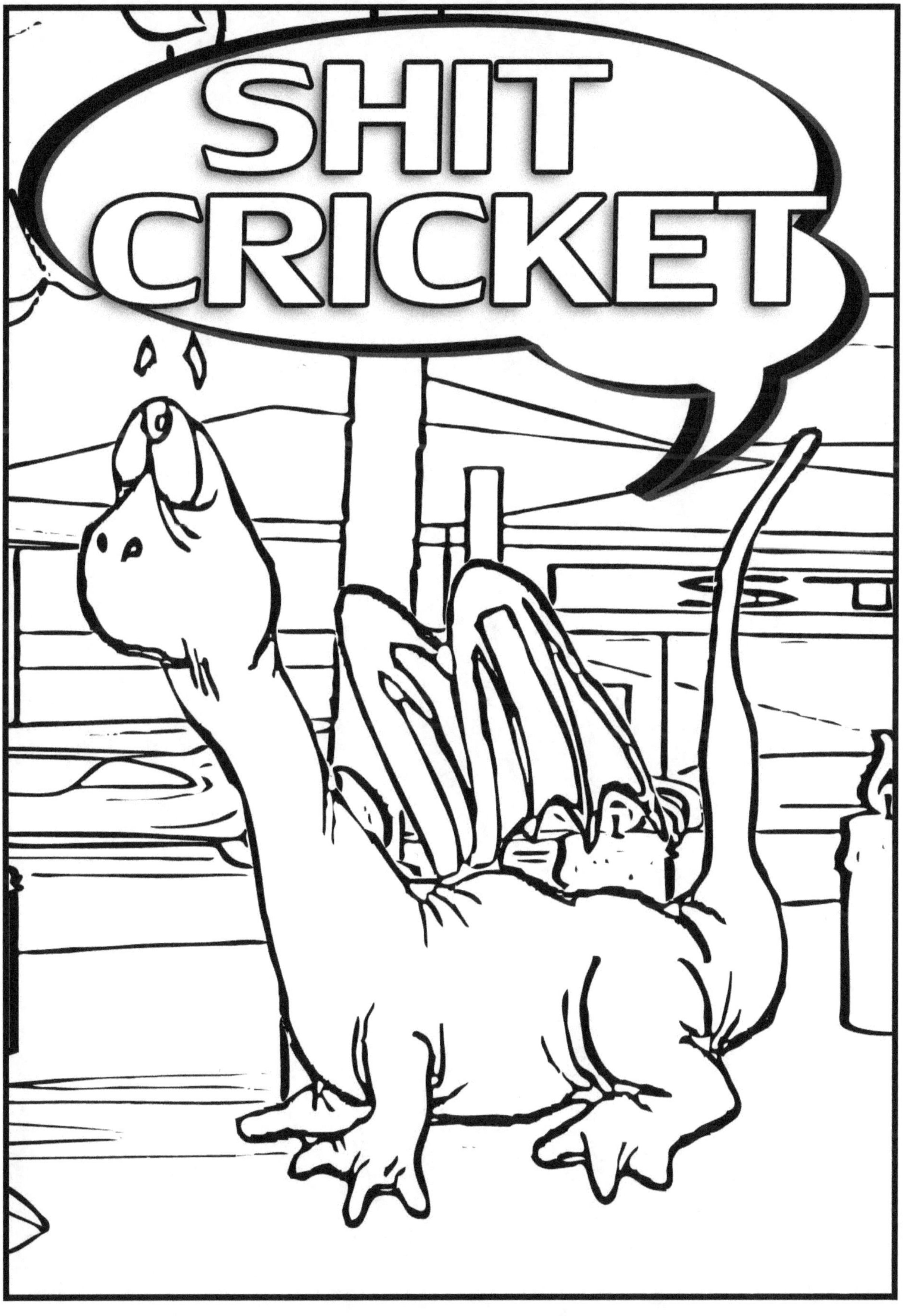
SHIT CRICKET

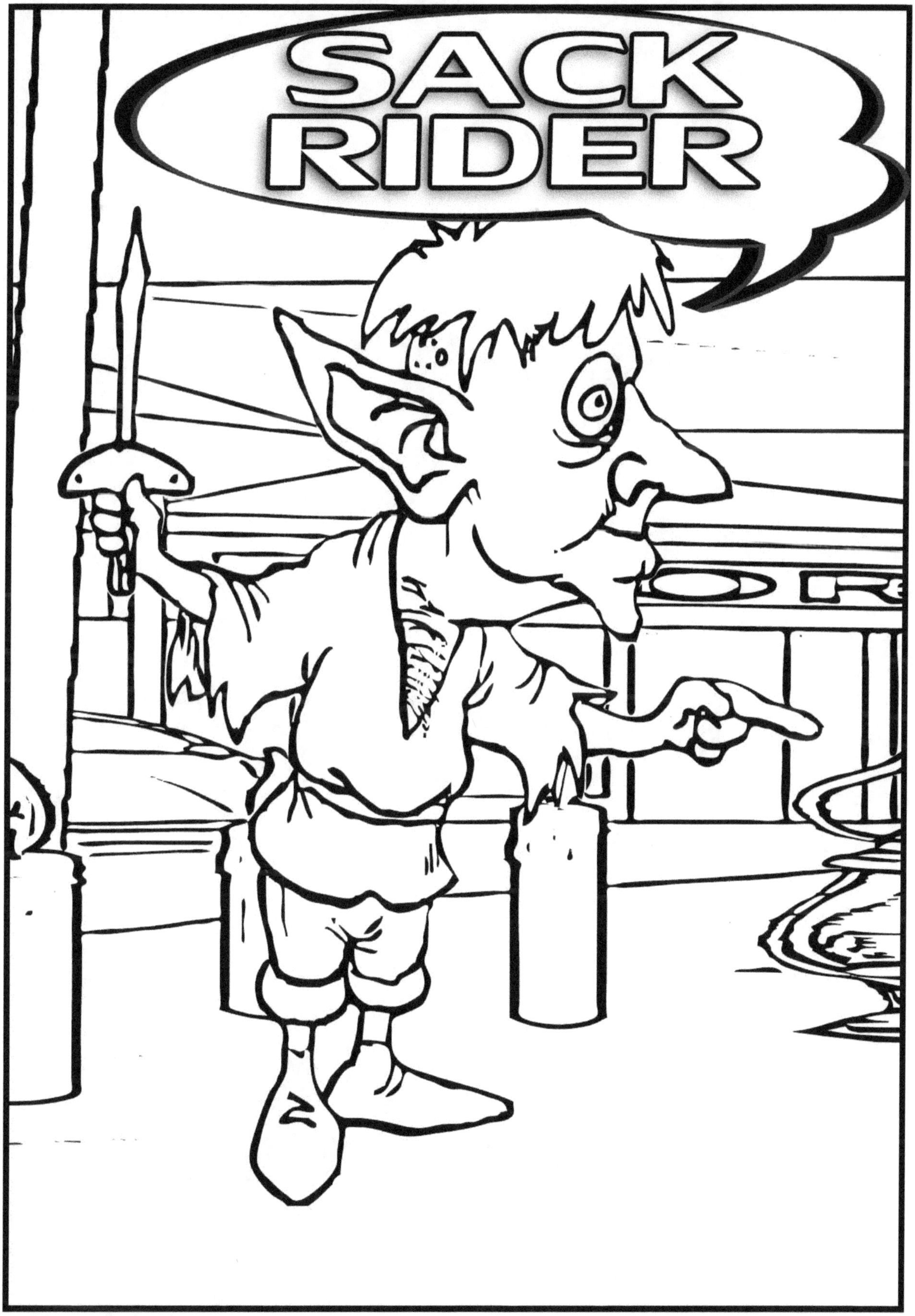
SACK
RIDER

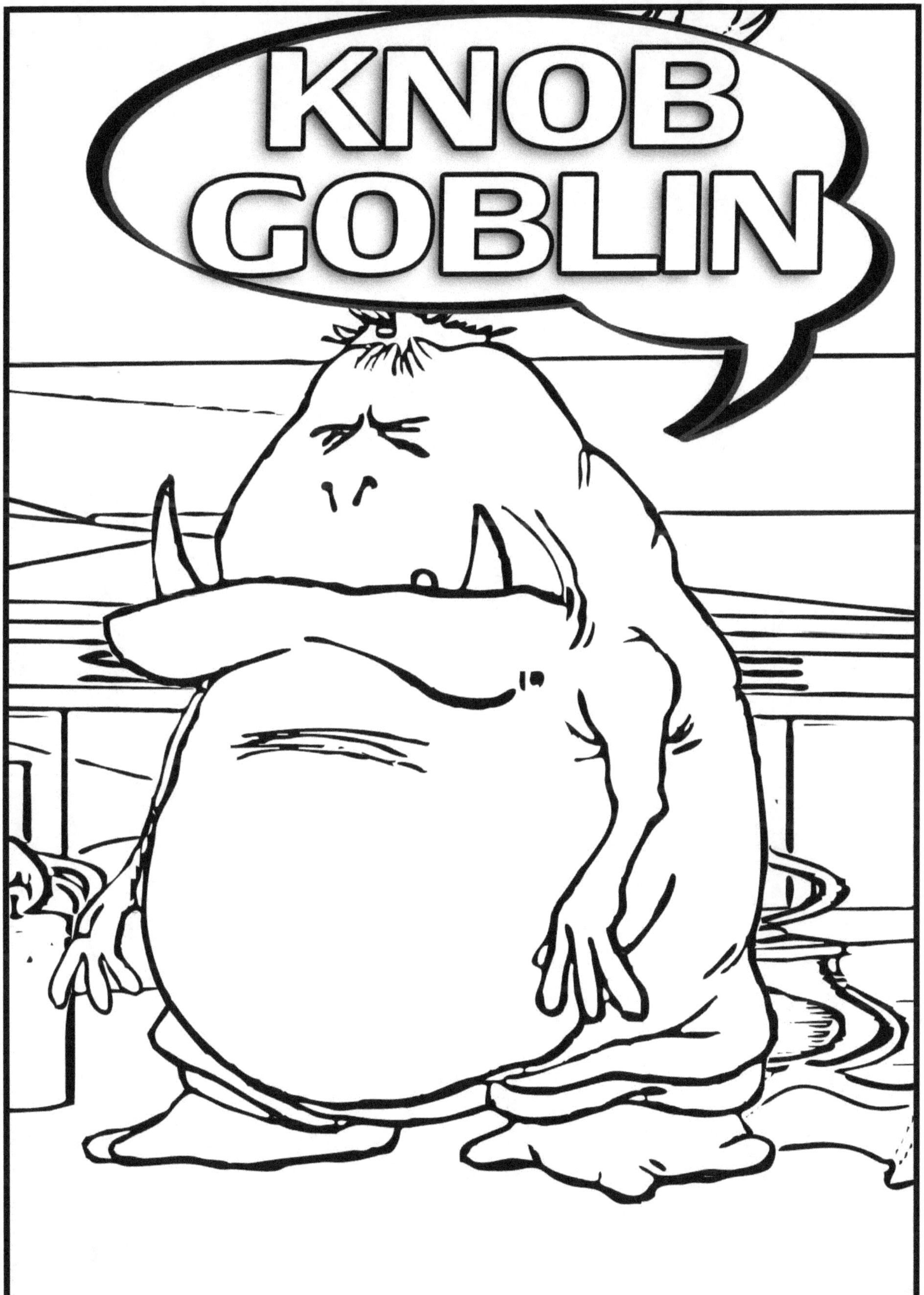
KNOB GOBLIN

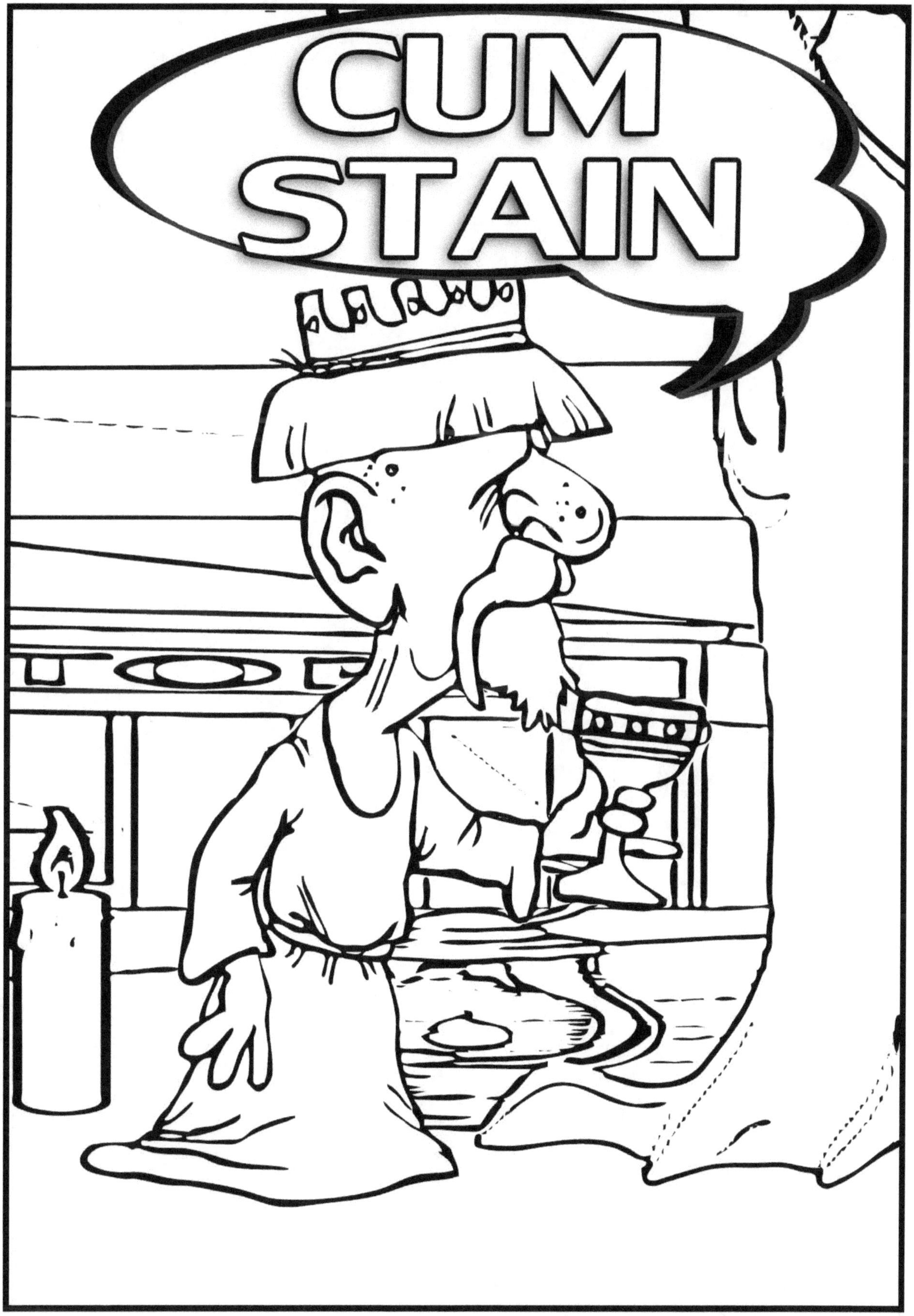
CUM STAIN

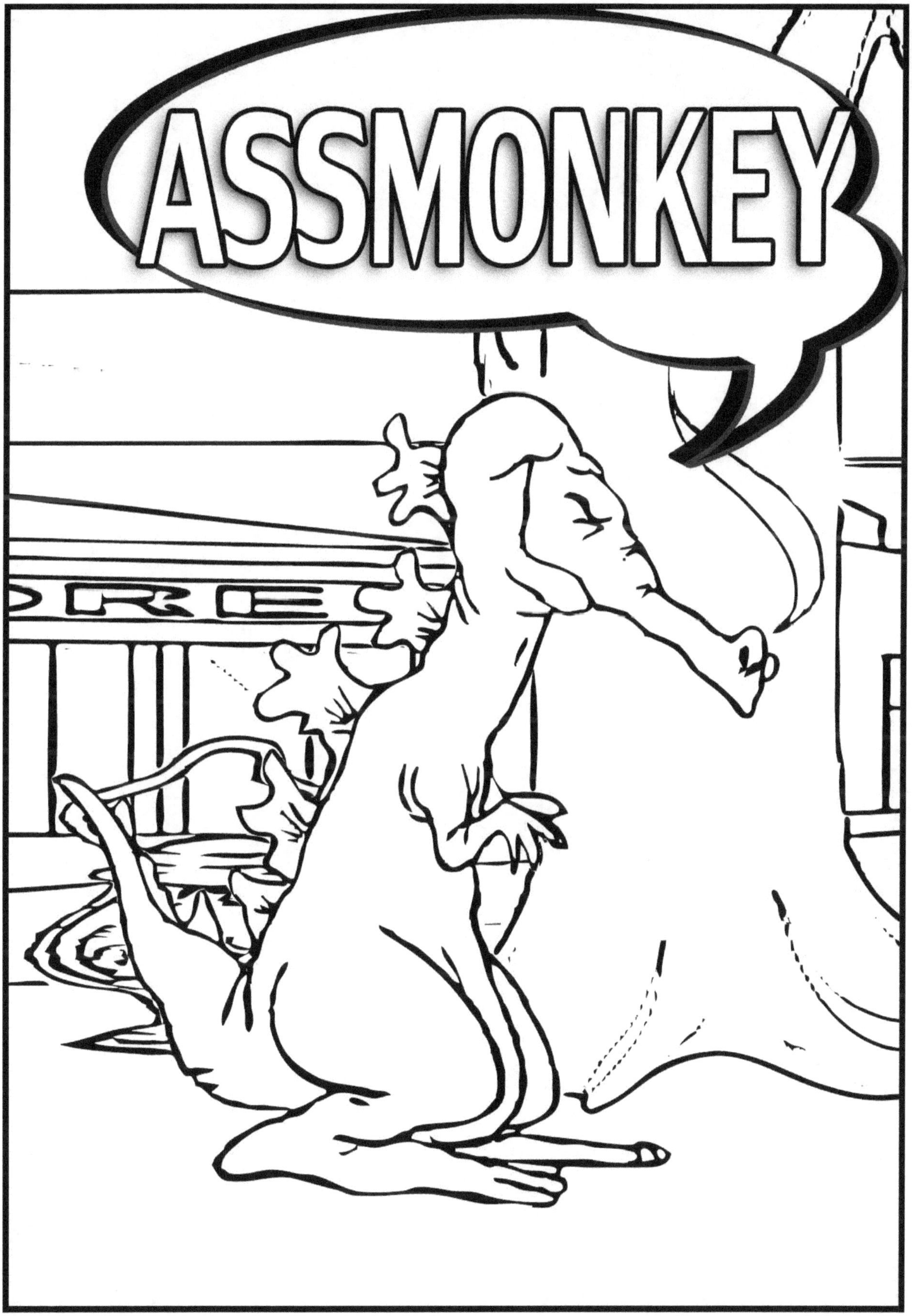
ASSMONKEY

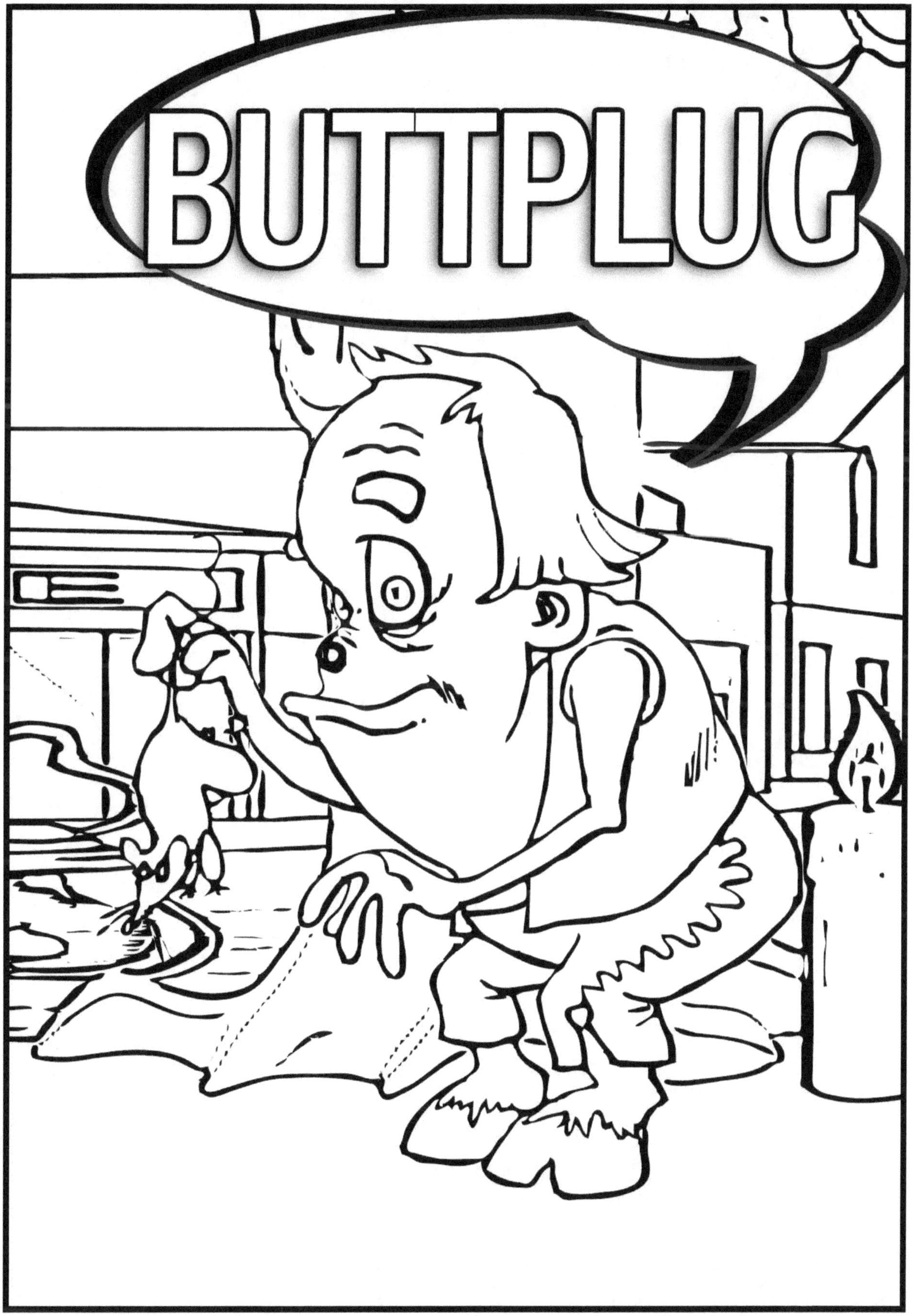
BUTTPLUG

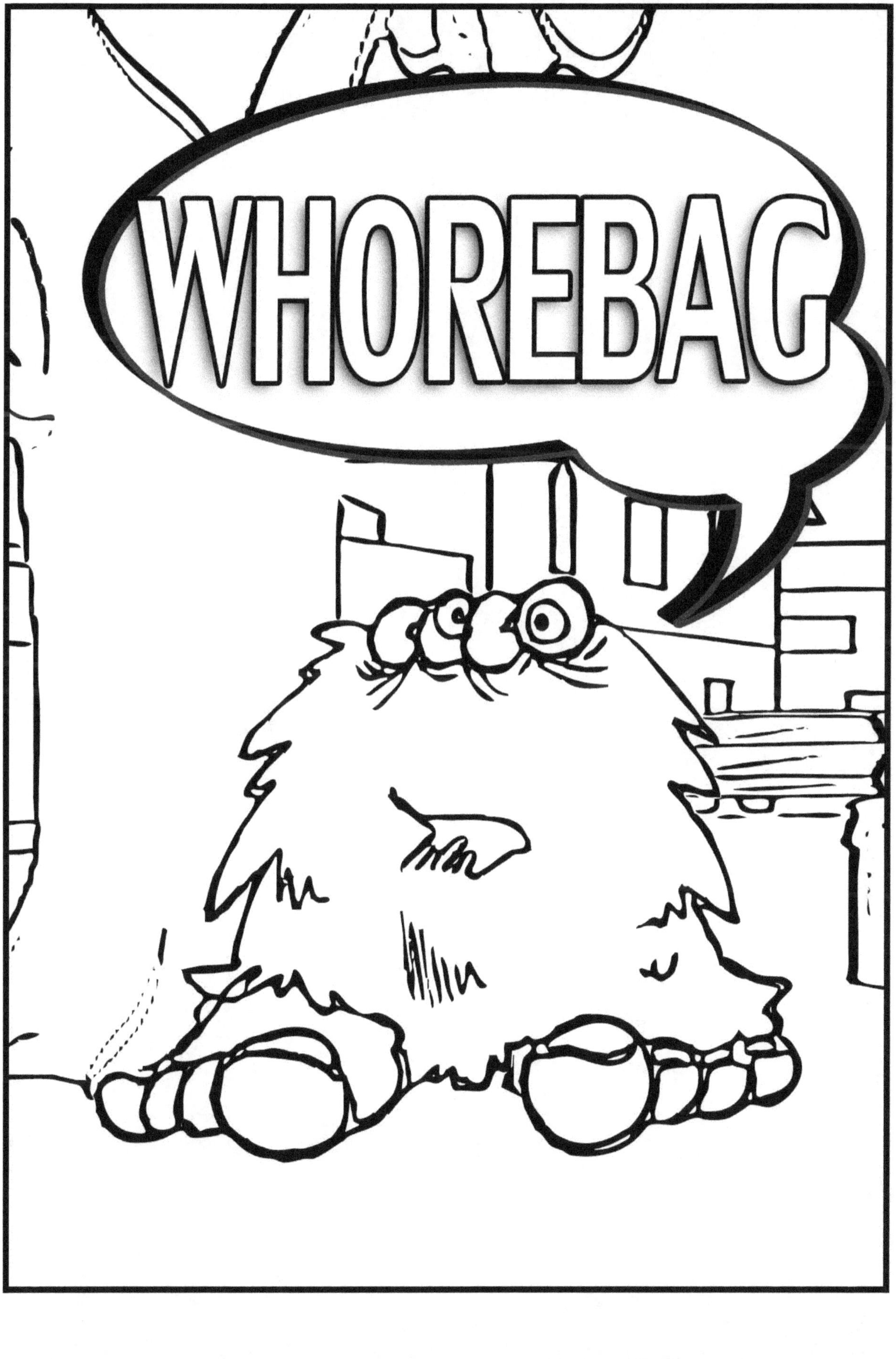
WHOREBAG

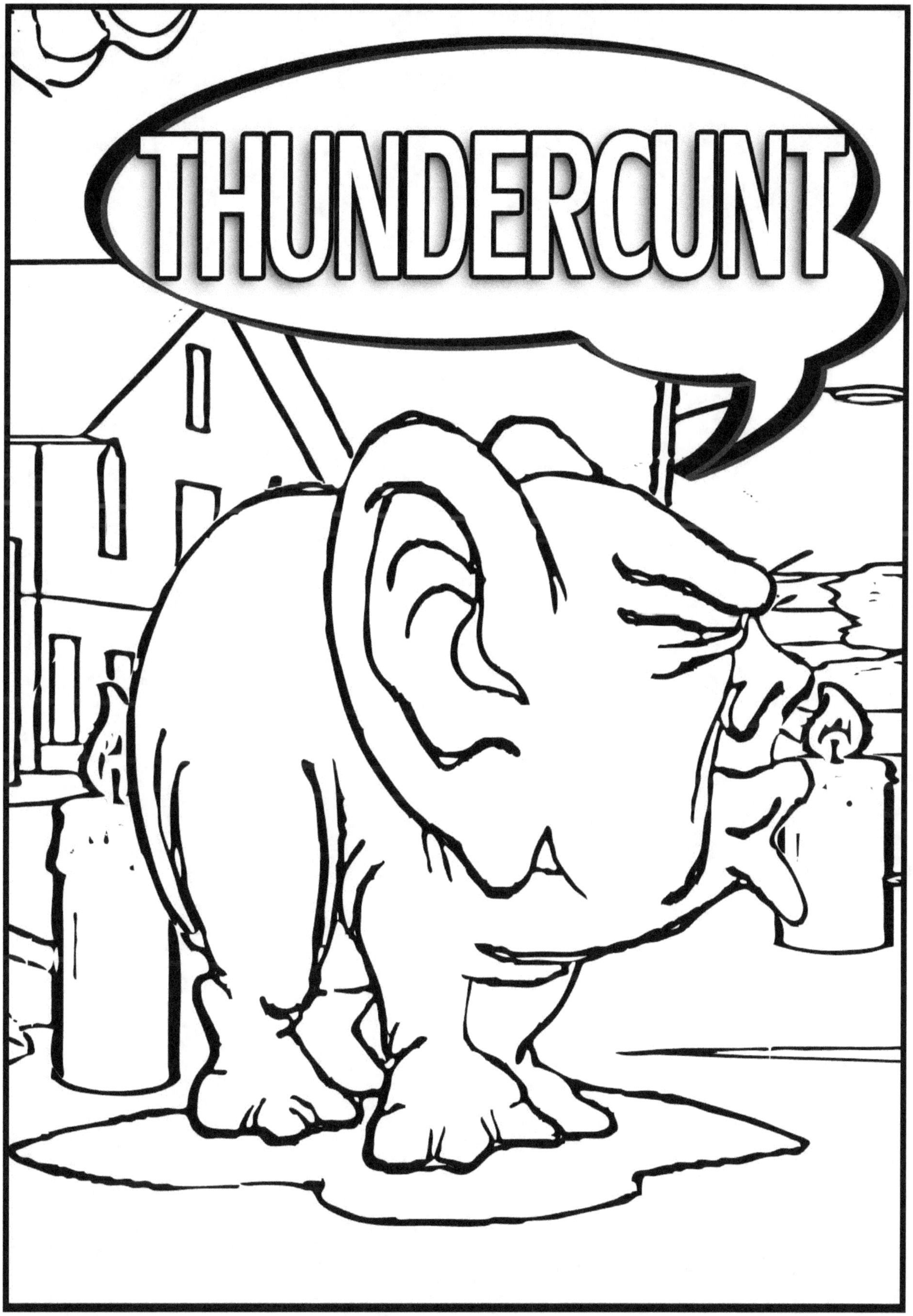
THUNDERCUNT

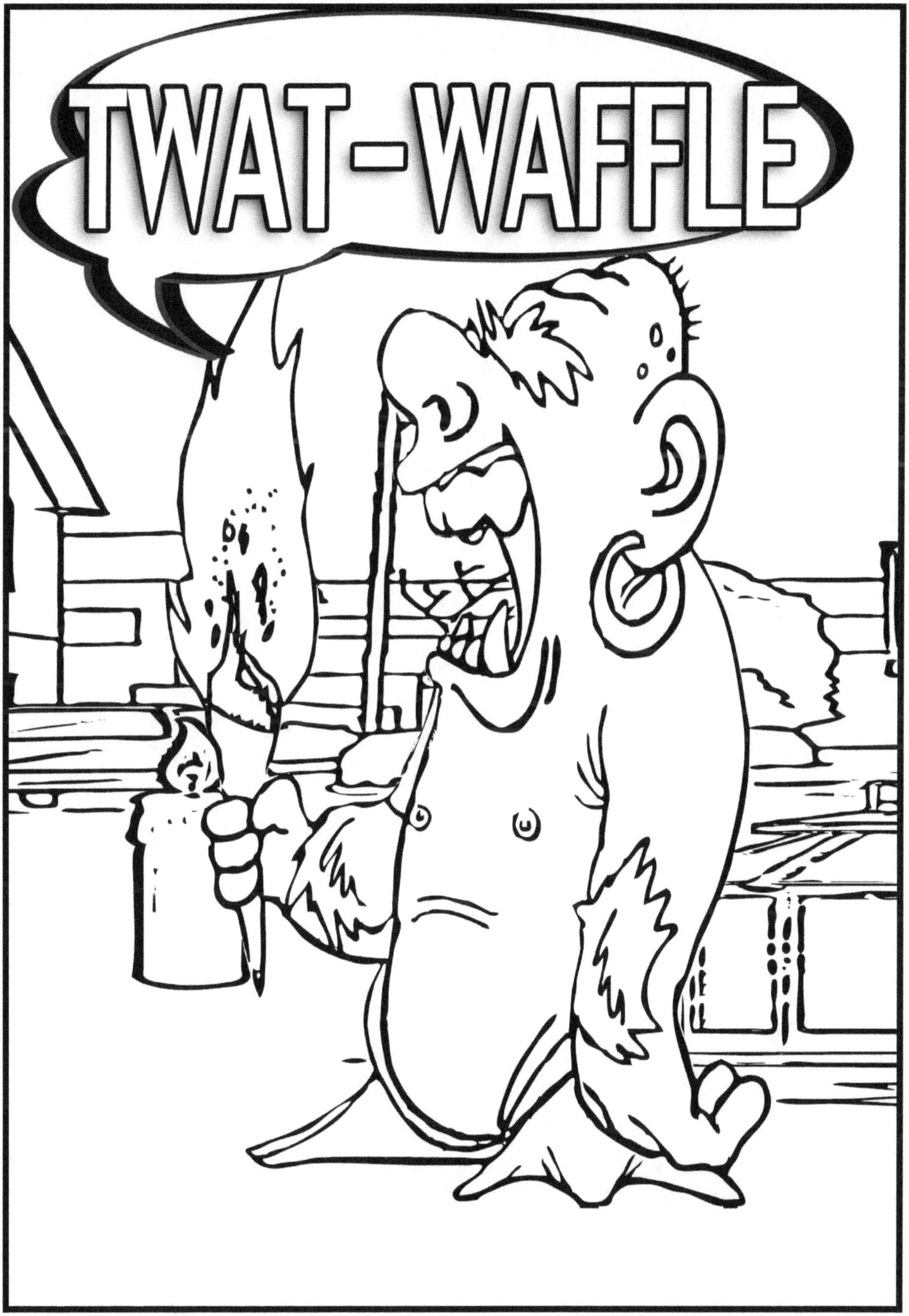
TWAT-WAFFLE

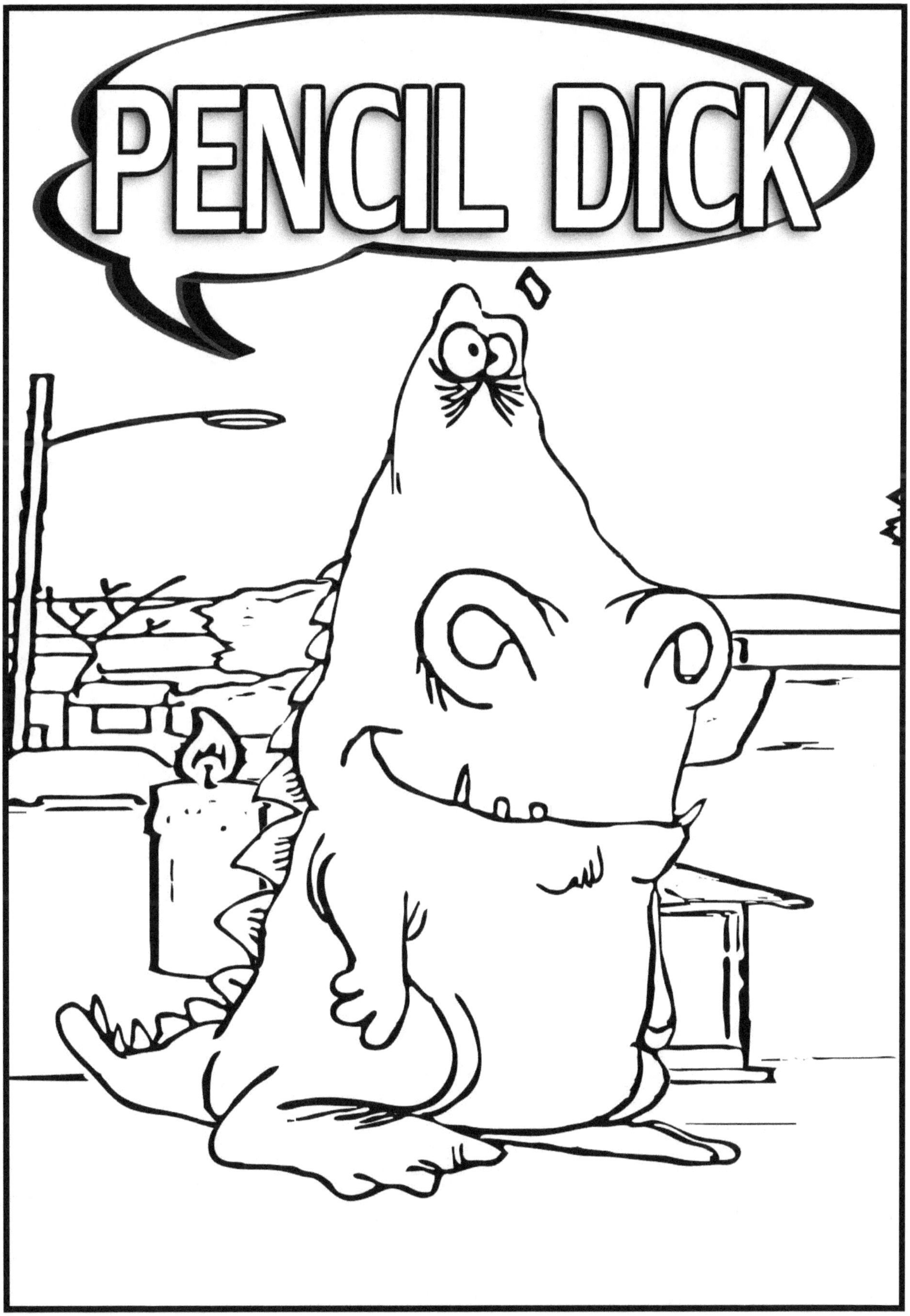
PENCIL DICK

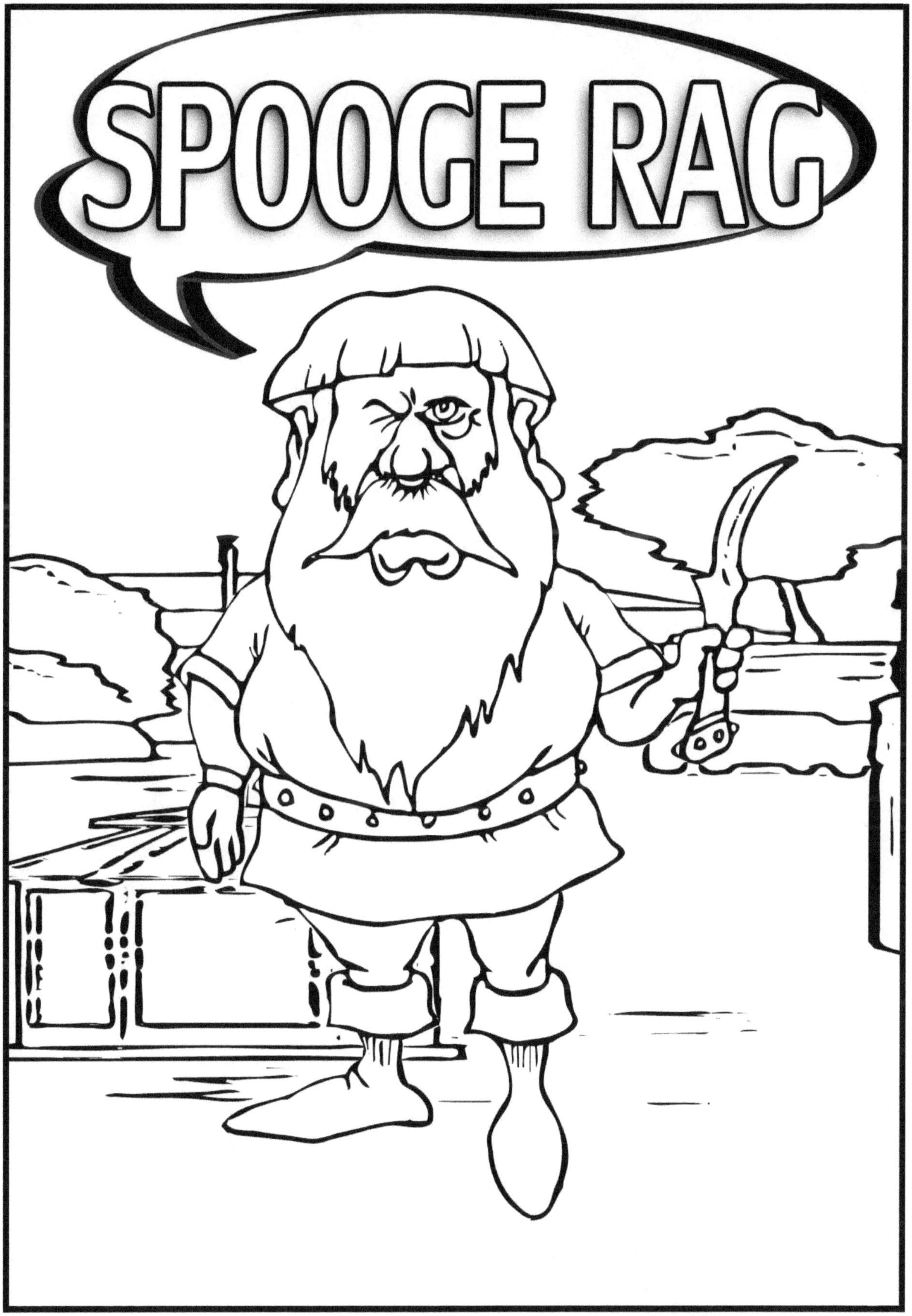
SPOOGE RAG

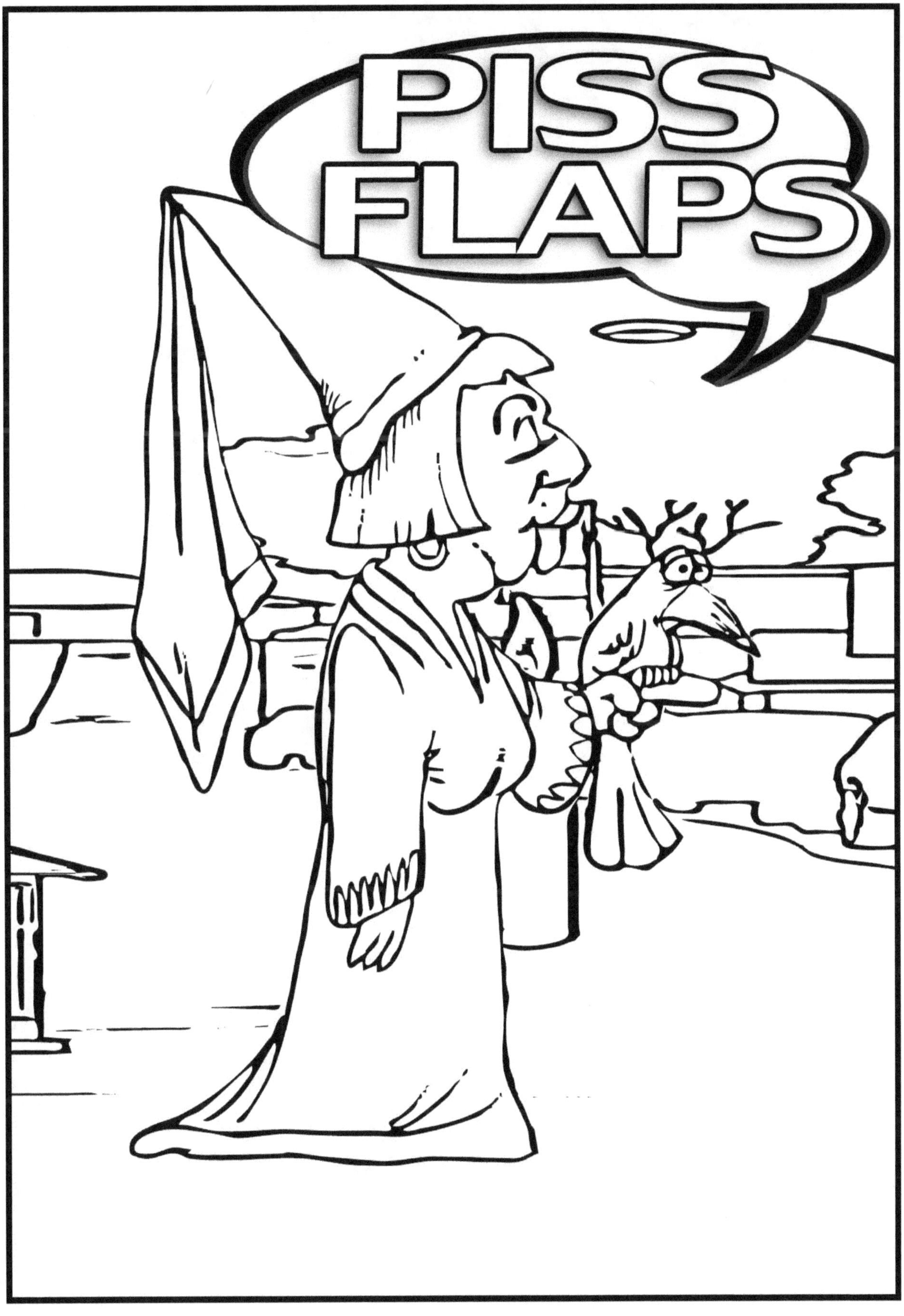
PISS FLAPS

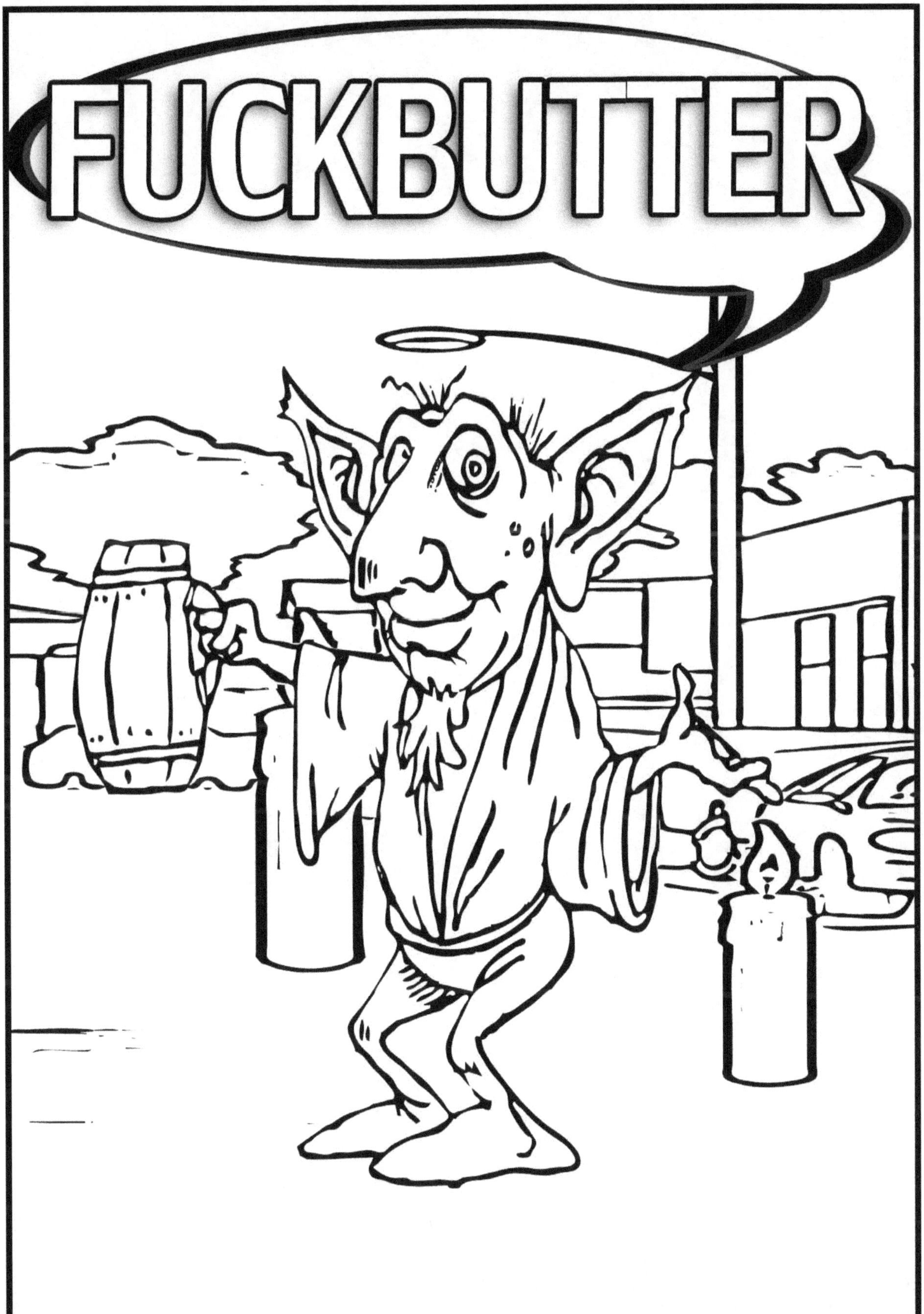
FUCKBUTTER

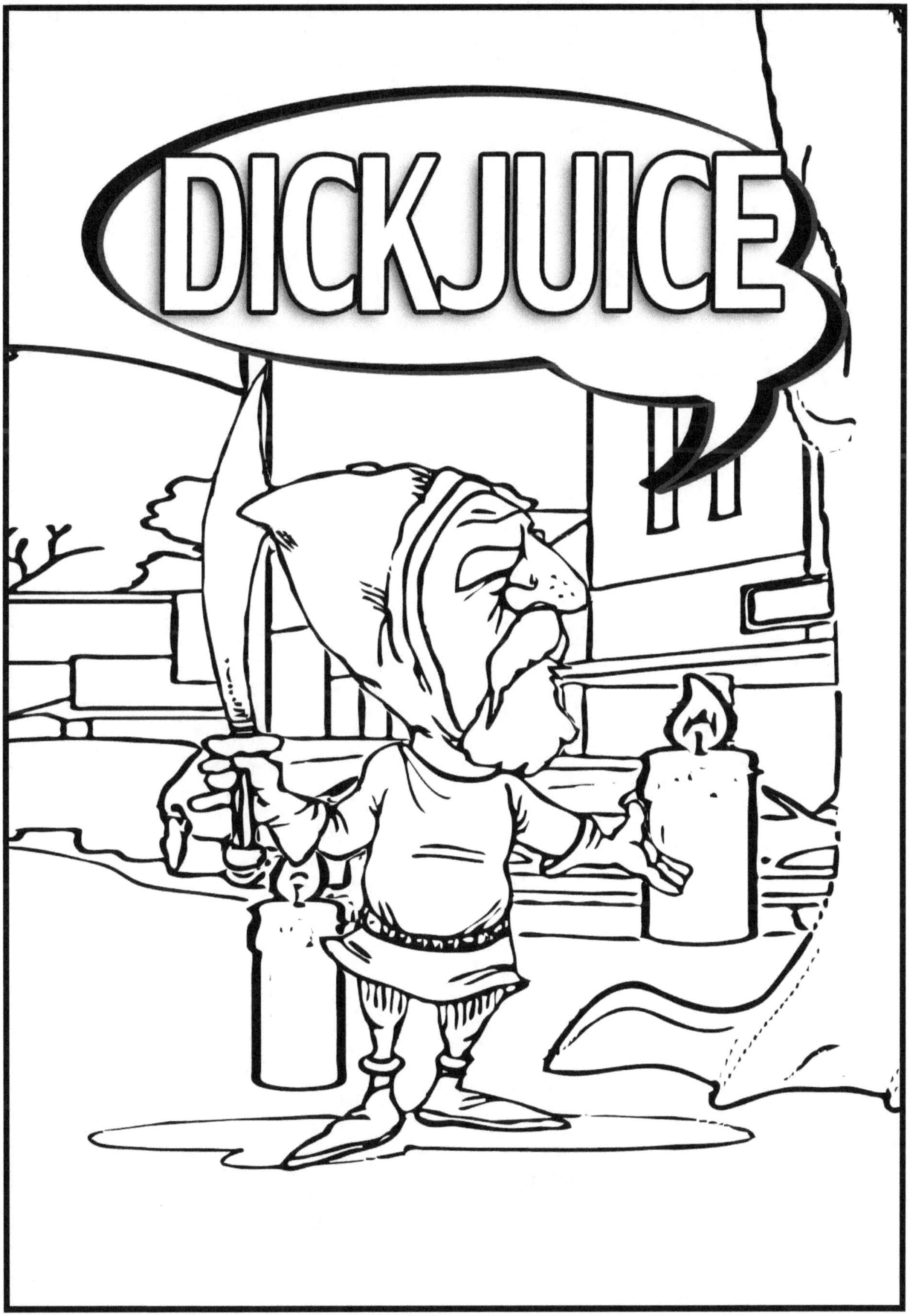
DICKJUICE

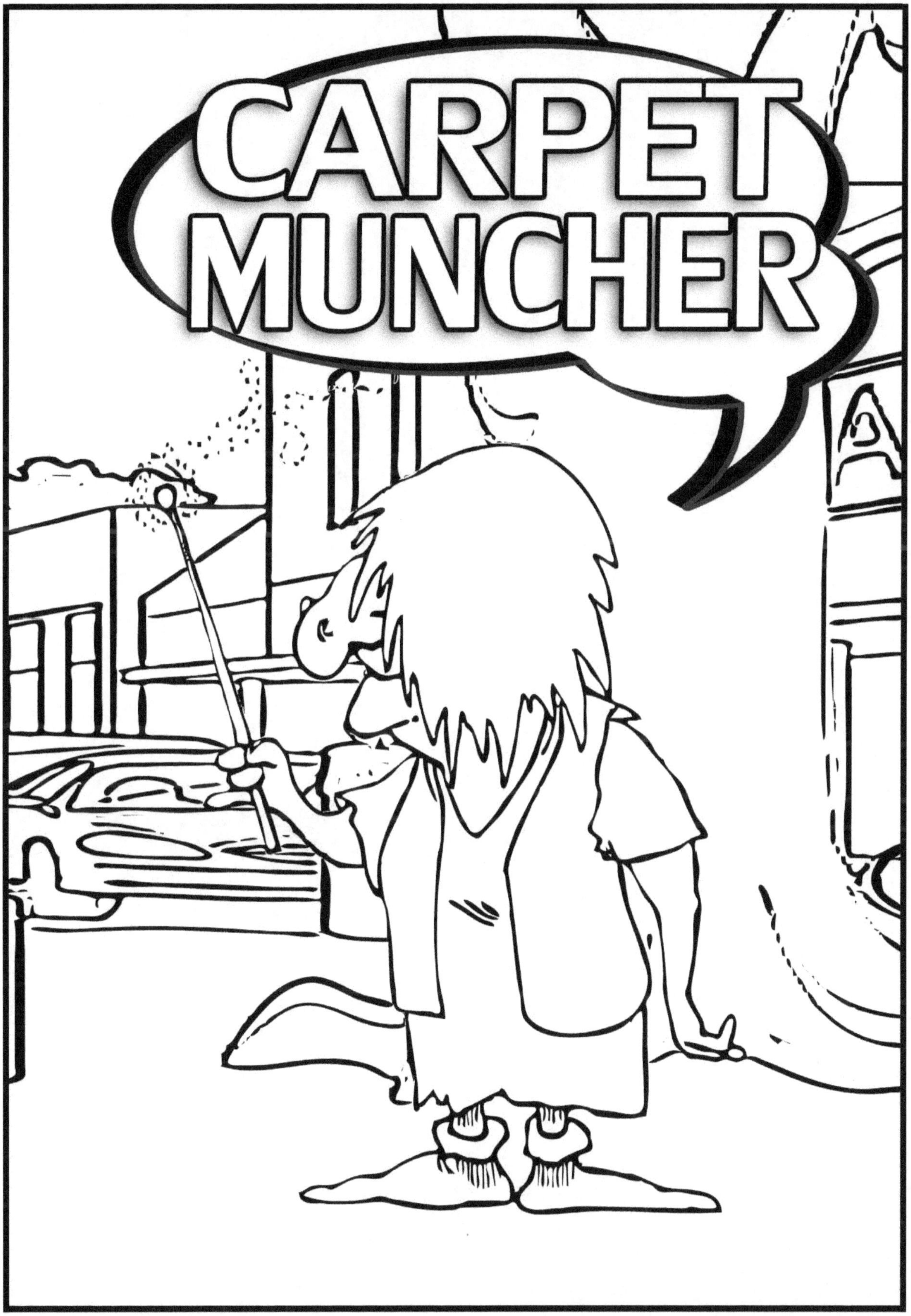
CARPET MUNCHER

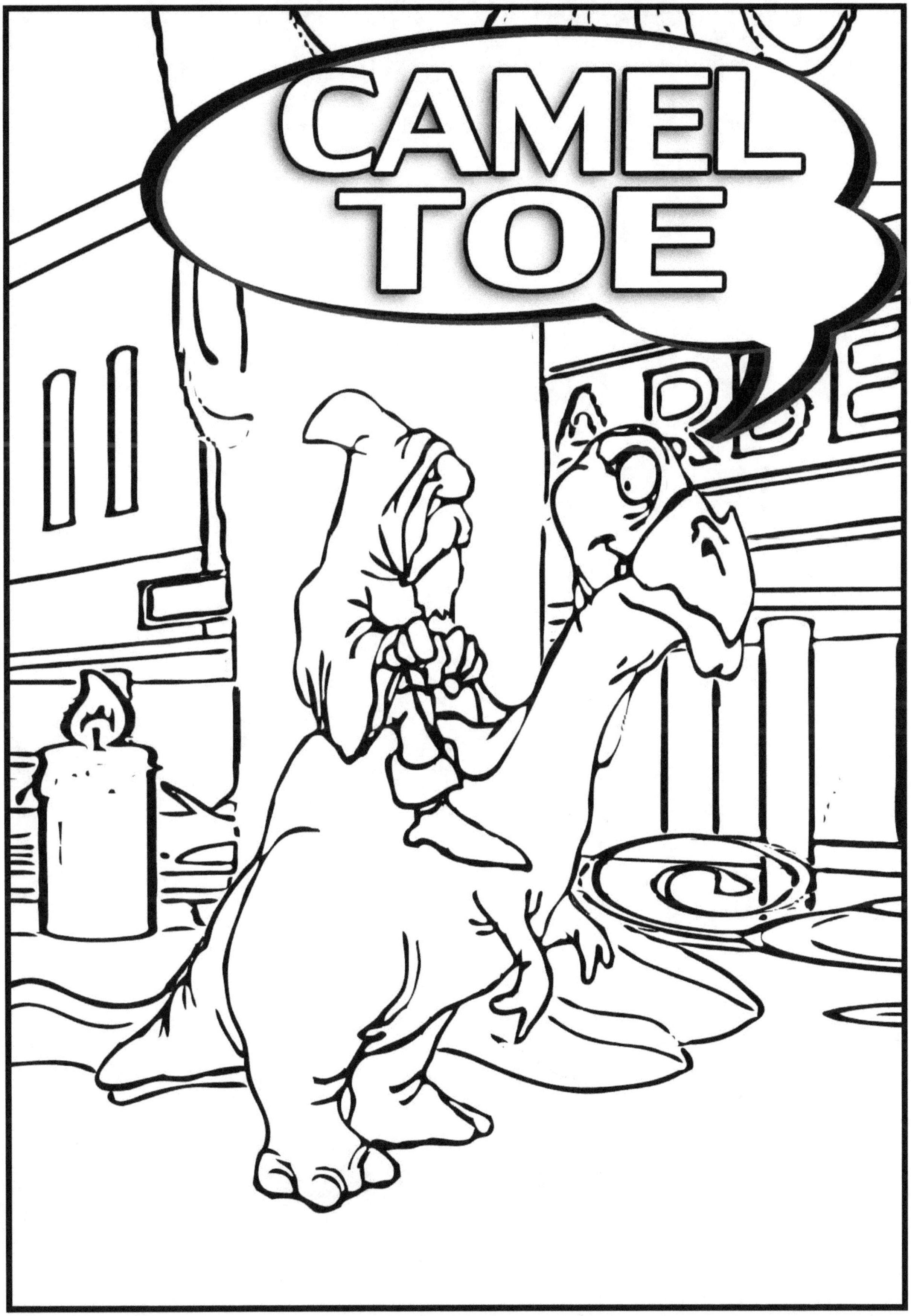
CAMEL TOE

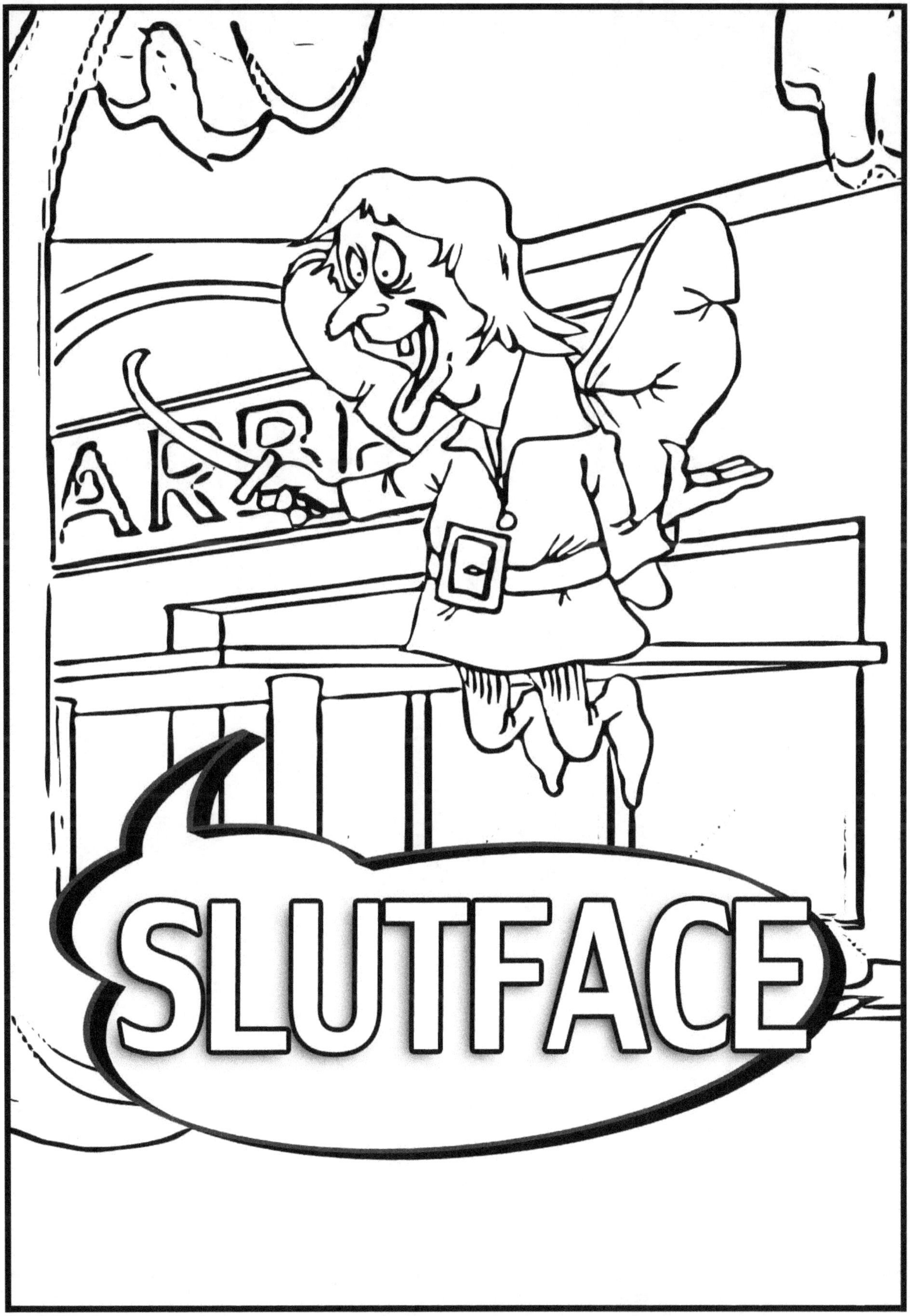
SLUTFACE

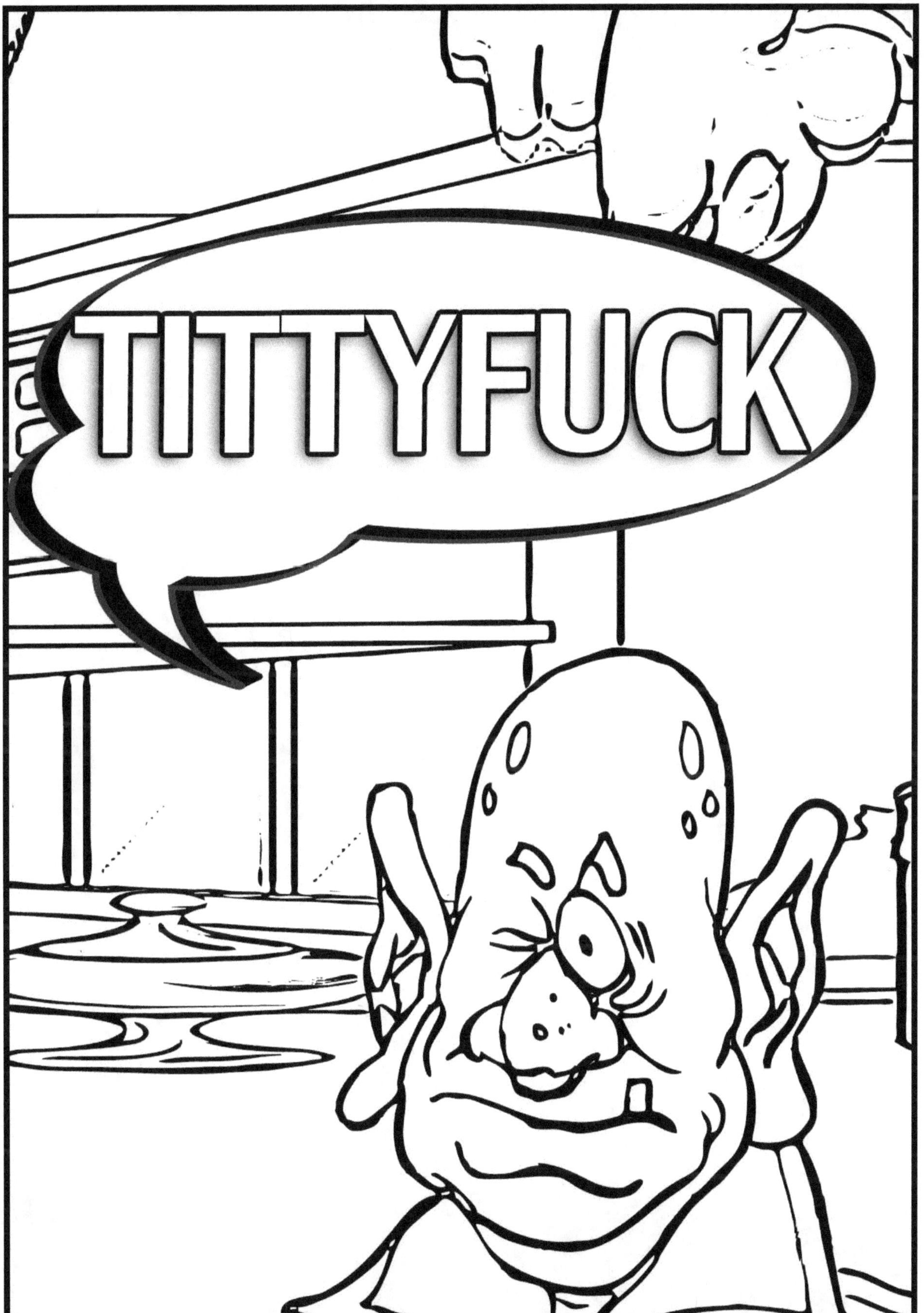
TITTYFUCK

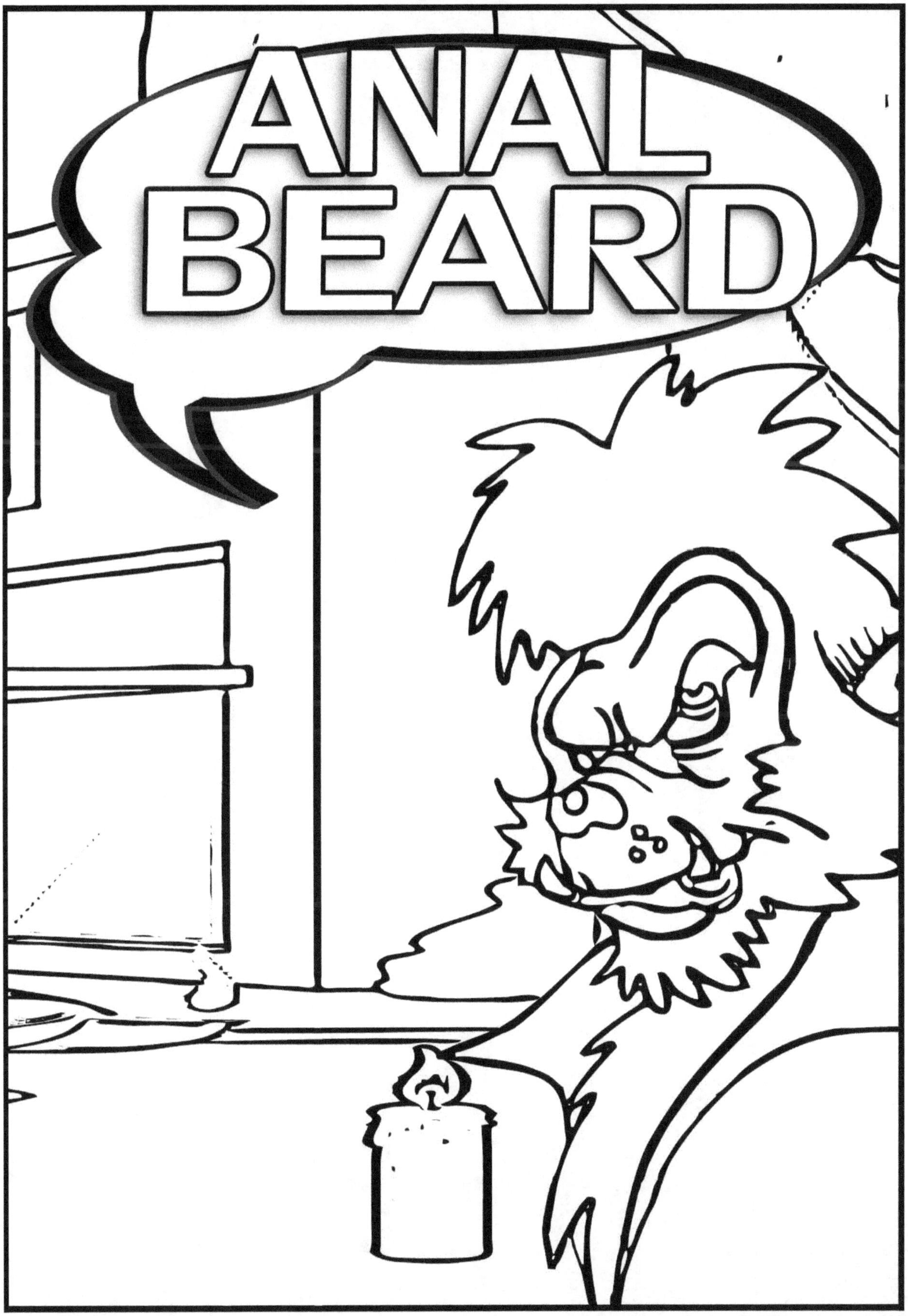
ANAL BEARD

www.ingramcontent.com/pod-product-compliance
Lightning Source LLC
Chambersburg PA
CBHW080612190526
45169CB00007B/2987
* 9 7 8 1 5 2 3 7 4 4 3 9 8 *